A Strong Man

First Edition
05 04 03 02 01   5 4 3 2 1

Published by
Gibbs Smith, Publisher
P.O. Box 667
Layton, Utah 84041

Order toll-free: (1-800) 748-5439
Website: _www.gibbs-smith.com_
E-mail: _info@gibbs-smith.com_

Edited by Suzanne Taylor
Designed and produced by J. Scott Knudsen, Park City, Utah
Printed and bound in China

Library of Congress Cataloging-in-Publication Data
Pearson, Carol Lynn.
   A strong man : a fable for our times / by Carol Lynn Pearson ;
   illustrated by Kathleen Peterson.—1st ed.
      p. cm.
   ISBN 1-58685-073-3
   I. Title.

PS3566.E227 S76   2001
   813'.54—dc21

                    00-011748

A Strong Man

a fable for our times

Carol Lynn Pearson

ILLUSTRATED BY

Kathleen Peterson

GIBBS·SMITH
P
PUBLISHER

SALT LAKE CITY

For my sons, John and Aaron—thanks for your strength.
C.L.P.

For my sons, Alex and Eric—thanks for your strength.
K.P.

There was a man. He was a good, strong man, and everyone who saw him admired his abilities.

One day the Chief said, "You are a very fast runner. I need your feet to run up the mountain and through the forest and across the grassy plain. I need you to kill the deer and the pigs and bring them back to our cave so that our women and our children may have food. Give us your feet."

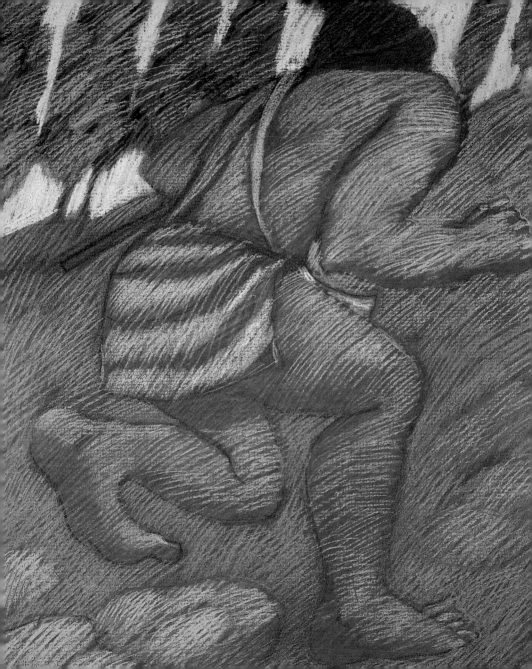

Sometimes, after a long day of running and bringing back food, the man sat and wearily stared at the fire. Something within him felt as lifeless as the carcass that sizzled and spat. He wondered if there might be more to him than the swiftness of his feet.

But he saw that it was true, they needed to eat. And it was good when the Chief smiled and nodded. So the man gave his feet and he gave them well. He ran up many mountains and through many forests and across many plains.

For he was a strong man, and, after all, isn't that what a man does?

One day, as the man came running in with a fat goat over his shoulders, the Pharaoh said to him, "You have a very strong back. I need your back to bring the cedars in from Lebanon and to place the stones for the Great Pyramid and to haul water from the rivers. Give me your back."

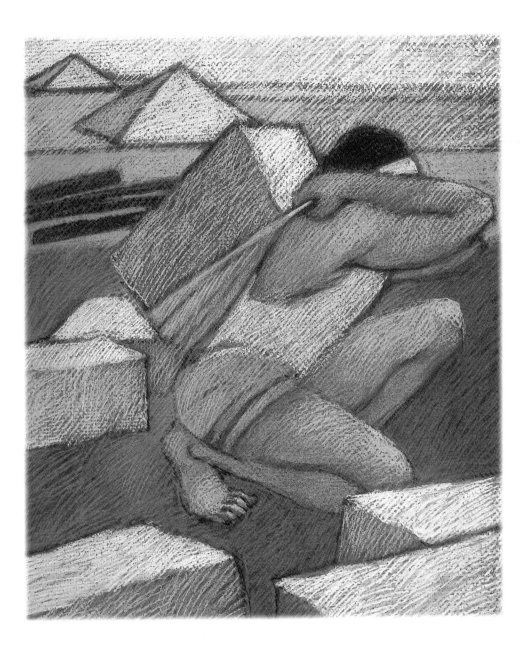

Often, after a hard day of pushing and pulling and hauling, the man felt very, very tired, and as empty inside as a newly carved tomb. He wondered if there might be more to him than the strength of his back.

But he saw that the Great Pyramid did indeed need building, and he observed too that the whip was very painful. And so he gave his back and he gave it well.

For he was a strong man, and, after all, isn't that what a man does?

One day, as the man came in from a very hard day in the galley, the King said to him, "Look! The enemy is at our borders. I need your strong arms to carry this lance—this rifle—this bayonet—this parachute—this napalm. Give me your arms!"

Sometimes, after a full day of killing the Visigoths and burning the heretics and bombing the enemy, the man wondered if there might be more to him than the strength of his arms. As he stared at the night sky, something in his center felt as dark as ash and as cold as steel.

But he saw that the enemy was indeed at the borders, and he had learned not to cross the King. So he gave his arms and he gave them well.

For he was a strong man, and, after all, isn't that what a man does?

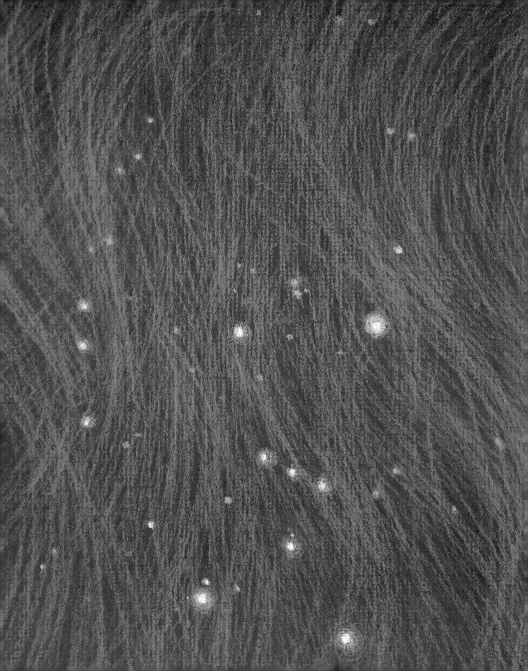

One day, as the man came limping home from Vietnam, the Boss met him at the door and said, "Quick! The company lost $60 million in the last quarter. And the recent leveraged buyout was a bust. And the bank called in the loan on the property in the Bahamas. You are a kick-butt kind of a guy. I need a workable plan by 3:45. Give me your brain, your brain, your brain!"

And so the man gave his brain and he saved the casinos in the Bahamas, and he gave his brain the next day and the next. Often he did not sleep at all, and there seemed always to be something dark between him and the sun, and he wondered if there might not be more to him than his brain.

But he saw that it was indeed necessary to account and merge and estimate and negotiate and bid, for he needed to pay the mortgage and take the kids to Disneyland, and he would love to get that promotion. And so he gave his brain and he gave it well.

For he was a strong man, and, after all, isn't that what a man does?

All day long and often into the night, the man ran and he pushed and he carried and he planned and he went to bed. And then he got up and once again he ran and he pushed and he carried and he planned. And when he went to bed and when he got up, he felt very tired and very old and very empty.

One day the man came home totally depleted from long hours of tracking consumer sentiment. And a woman who loved him said, "You know what? I've been thinking. Look what we have done to our world. The earth is sad and the children are crying. The women are disillusioned and the men are confused. You are a strong man. Give us your heart."

"**W**e need your heart so that you can hold the little ones, clean up the rivers and the oceans, regrow the forests, make the food safe, and stop the wars. We need your heart to help heal all the fractures and the sorrow and the pain. We need your heart so your son can grow up whole and your daughter can grow up free. I need your heart so that when I look into your eyes I can see who we really are. **You** need your heart so you will have a place to put the love we give you."

The man looked around and saw that it was so. He looked within and saw that it was so. He placed his hands over his heart and felt something move. The weariness and the darkness and the cold went away, and his center filled with something warm that spread and spilled out from his eyes.

"Ah, yes," said the woman. "Ah, yes."

And so the man gave his heart. It came out through feet that knew just where to walk and how to stand strong, through a back that knew which burdens to lift and how, through hands that knew how to heal and what to give, and through a mind that birthed a vision of a bright future.

The earth greened and the children grew up laughing. The women believed again and the men found joy. There was food on the table, and friend and enemy sat down to supper. When the man slept there was a smile on his face. When he got up in the morning he listened to the voice, and the voice now was his own, and the voice said, "Today, give your heart." And so he did, and he gave it well. That day and the next day and the next.

For he was a strong man . . .

. . . And, after all, that is what a man does.